D0953745

Red Foxes

by Ruth Strother

Consultant:
Blaire Van Valkenburgh
Professor
UCLA Department of Ecology and Evolutionary Biology

BEARPORT
PUBLISHING

New York, New York

Credits

Cover and Title Page, © Tony Northrup/Shutterstock; 4–5, © Carolina K. Smith MD/Shutterstock; 6–7, 8–9, © iStockphoto/Thinkstock; 10, © Stock Connection/SuperStock; 10–11, © Betty Shelton/Shutterstock; 12, © Denis Pepin/Shutterstock; 12–13, © NHPA/SuperStock; 14, © Scenic Shutterbug/Shutterstock; 14–15, © Glen Gaffney/Shutterstock; 16, © Menno Schaefer/Shutterstock; 16–17, © NHPA/SuperStock; 18–19, © Animals Animals/SuperStock; 20–21, © Gerard Lacz Images/SuperStock; 22T, © iStockphoto/Thinkstock; 22B, © Pakul54/Shutterstock; 23T, © Pim Leijen/Shutterstock; 23B, © Denis Pepin/Shutterstock.

Publisher: Kenn Goin
Senior Editor: Joyce Tavolacci
Creative Director: Spencer Brinker
Design: Candice Madrid
Photo Researcher: Arnold Ringstad

Library of Congress Cataloging-in-Publication Data

Strother, Ruth.
  Red foxes / by Ruth Strother ; consultant, Blaire Van Valkenburgh.
      p. cm. — (Wild canine pups)
  Includes bibliographical references and index.
  ISBN-13: 978-1-61772-927-0 (library binding) — ISBN-10: 1-61772-927-2 (library binding)
  1. Red fox—Infancy—Juvenile literature. 2. Foxes—Infancy—Juvenile literature. I.
Van Valkenburgh, Blaire. II. Title.
  QL737.C22S786 2014
  599.775—dc23
                                    2013011046

Copyright © 2014 Bearport Publishing Company, Inc. All rights reserved. No part of this publication may be reproduced in whole or in part, stored in any retrieval system, or transmitted in any form or by any means, electronic, mechanical, photocopying, recording, or otherwise, without written permission from the publisher.

For more information, write to Bearport Publishing Company, Inc., 45 West 21st Street, Suite 3B, New York, New York 10010. Printed in the United States of America.

10 9 8 7 6 5 4 3 2 1

❧ Contents ❧

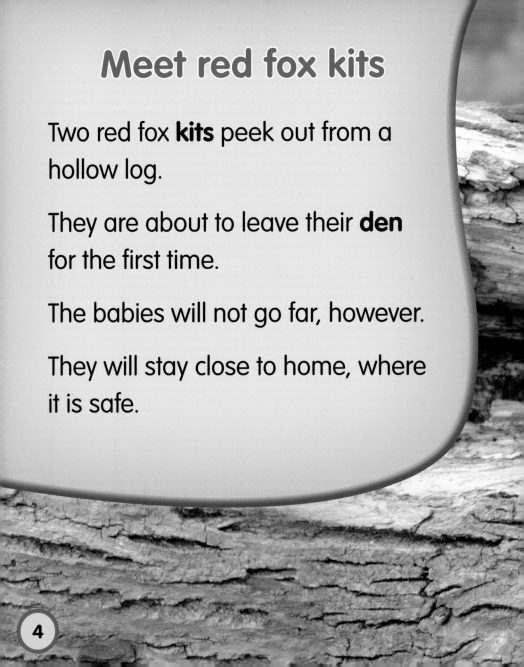

Meet red fox kits

Two red fox **kits** peek out from a hollow log.

They are about to leave their **den** for the first time.

The babies will not go far, however.

They will stay close to home, where it is safe.

red fox kits

What is a red fox?

Red foxes belong to a group of animals called **canines**.

Red foxes have pointed ears and noses.

Adults have red fur and bushy tails.

Adult red fox size

bushy tail

When the foxes sleep, they wrap their tails around their bodies to stay warm.

pointed ears

Where do red foxes live?

Red foxes live in many different parts of the world.

They make their homes in forests, in deserts, and even near cities.

North America

Europe   Asia

Atlantic Ocean

Africa

Pacific Ocean

South America

Indian Ocean

Australia

Southern Ocean

N
W   E
S

Antarctica

☐ **Where red foxes live**

red fox
in forest

Fox family

Foxes live alone or in small family groups.

Sometimes the family includes two parents and their grown female kits.

The older kits help raise the family's new kits.

older kit

younger kit

red fox
family

Home sweet home

In spring, a female fox often makes several dens.

In one of the dens, she gives birth to up to nine tiny kits.

The mother watches and listens for **predators**, such as coyotes.

coyote

If an enemy comes near, she will move her kits to a safer den.

den

mother fox

kit

Newborn kits

Red fox kits are born with gray fur.

Over time, their fur will turn red like their mother's.

kit with
gray fur

When they are first born, the kits drink milk from their mother's body.

The milk helps them grow stronger each day.

kits drinking milk from mother

Playing and eating

When the kits are three weeks old, they begin to play with each other.

Playing helps them learn to hunt.

Before they begin to hunt, however, their father brings them meat.

He feeds them mice, birds, and other small animals.

adult bringing meat to kits

kits playing

Time to explore

When the kits are five weeks old, they leave the den area.

However, the adults still watch over them to keep them safe.

At three months of age, the kits begin hunting mice on their own.

father fox
watching over kit

All grown up

After six months, the kits are full-grown adults.

Some of the females stay with their parents.

However, most will leave their family to raise their own tiny kits!

grown-up
red fox

Glossary

canines (KAY-nyenz) members of the dog family, which includes pet dogs, wolves, and red foxes

den (DEN) a home where wild animals can rest, hide from enemies, and have babies

kits (KITS)
baby red foxes

predators (PRED-uh-turz)
animals that hunt and
eat other animals

Index

Read more

Levine, Michelle. *Red Foxes (Pull Ahead Books).* Minneapolis, MN: Lerner (2004).

McDonald, Mary Ann. *Foxes.* Mankato, MN: Child's World (2008).

Murphy, Patricia J., and Gail Saunders-Smith. *Red Foxes.* Mankato, MN: Capstone (2004).

Learn more online

To learn more about red foxes, visit
www.bearportpublishing.com/WildCaninePups

About the author

Ruth Strother has written and edited numerous award-winning books for children and adults. She has spanned the United States, starting life in New York, growing up in Minnesota, and now living in Southern California with her husband, daughter, and black Lab. Her yard is frequently visited by coyotes and foxes.